Parents

by
Gail Saunders-Smith

Pebble Books
an imprint of Capstone Press

Pebble Books

Pebble Books are published by Capstone Press
818 North Willow Street, Mankato, Minnesota 56001
http://www.capstone-press.com
Copyright © 1998 by Capstone Press
All Rights Reserved • Printed in the United States of America

Library of Congress Cataloging-in-Publication Data
Saunders-Smith, Gail.
    Parents/by Gail Saunders-Smith.
    p.cm.
    Includes bibliographical references and index.
    Summary: Simple text and photographs describe
some of the ways parents help children, including
reading together, cooking, swimming, and dressing.
    ISBN 1-56065-492-9
    1. Parent and child--Juvenile literature.
2. Parents--Juvenile literature. [1. Parent and
child.] I. Title.

HQ755.85.S284 1997
306.874--dc21
                        97-23588
                          CIP
                          AC

Editorial Credits
Lois Wallentine, editor; James Franklin, design;
Michelle L. Norstad, photo research

Photo Credits
FPG/Dick Luria, cover, 16, 20; Dennie Cody, 4, 14;
    Cheryl Maeder, 6; Ron Chapple, 1, 10, 18; John
    Terence Turner, 12
Unicorn Stock/Rich Baker, 8

Table of Contents

Sometimes my mom
helps me swim.

Sometimes my mom
helps me learn.

Sometimes my mom
helps me skate.

Sometimes my dad
helps me dress.

Sometimes my dad
helps me ride.

Sometimes my dad
helps me hit.

Sometimes my mom and dad read with me.

Sometimes my mom and dad cook with me.

Sometimes my mom and dad walk with me.

Words to Know

cook—to prepare food for a meal

dress—to put on clothes

hit—to smack or strike at something

learn—to find out how to do something

read—to look at words and understand what they mean

ride—to travel on an animal or vehicle

skate—to glide or move along on a special type of boot that has wheels or a blade

swim—to move through the water without a boat

walk—to move along on your feet

Read More

Kaplan, John. *Mom and Me.* New York: Scholastic, 1996.

Morris, Ann. *The Daddy Book.* World's Family Series. Parsippany, N.J.: Silver Press, 1996.

Morris, Ann. *The Mommy Book.* World's Family Series. Parsipanny, N.J.: Silver Press, 1996.

Internet Sites

Family.com: Home Page
http://www.family.com

The Family Fun Network
http://www.ffn.org

Note to Parents and Teachers

This book describes the various ways parents help children. The clear photographs support beginning readers in making and maintaining the meaning of the text. The noun and verb changes are depicted in the photographs. Children may need assistance in using the Table of Contents, Words to Know, Internet Sites, and Index/Word List sections of this book.

Index/Word List

Word Count: 60
Early-Intervention Level: 4